LONDON MIDLAND
STEAM ON SHED
AF593721
SOUTHERN
STEAM IN ACTION
BORDERS STEAM
LIGHT RAILWAYS
standard gauge and narrow gauge
OF BRITAIN
ARTICULATED LOCOMOTIVES OF THE WORLD
MAIN LINE STEAM
STEAM IN india
SCOTTISH RAILWAYS
in the heyday of steam
GREAT WESTERN
STEAM THROUGH THE YEARS
WESTERNS
SUPERPOWER STEAM
ROUND THE WORLD
BRITISH TRAMS
SCOTTISH
BRANCH LINE STEAM
THE MIDLAND RAILWAY
the later years of
LMSR LOCOMOTIVES
GREAT WESTERN
a pictorial history

SOUTHERN BRANCH LINE STEAM: 3

30033
30033

SOUTHERN BRANCH LINE STEAM 3

TONY FAIRCLOUGH AND ALAN WILLS

D. BRADFORD BARTON LIMITED

Frontispiece: Drummond 'M7' 0-4-4T No.30033 hauls its train of L.S.W.R. stock along the Fawley branch near Hythe on 25 April 1953. [L. Elsey]

5088/3BL *ISBN 0 85153 383 3*

printed in Great Britain by Lovell Baines Print Ltd, Newbury, Berkshire

for the publishers

D. BRADFORD BARTON LTD · Trethellan House · Truro · Cornwall · England

introduction

The veteran driver gazed out of the cab of his equally elderly tank engine which was standing in the bay platform at the Junction with a waiting branch train. He was watching the hustle and bustle on the main line platform as the passengers boarded or descended from the London train which was making its brief call before hurrying on. Then came the guard's shrill whistling, his green flag waved and, with a thunderous roar, the 'West Country' at the head slipped her way eastwards. On passing the tank engine the main line driver exchanged a nod with our man who was following the Pacific's progress with just a pang of regret. For not so long ago he too had been a top link driver at one of the Southern's largest loco depots but when the vacancy had occurred at the small sub-shed on the branch he had decided to apply and was successful. Of course his duties were now very different. Three turns, early, middle and late were worked week by week on the short stretch of line which had now become very familiar indeed, a far cry from the many rosters covering a great deal of mileage over several main lines which had been his previous lot. But now he could plan his social life knowing exactly how the three duties would work out and there was no Sunday work to interrupt weekend activities. Again, the actual locomotive work was in complete contrast to his former handling of big Pacifics and 4-6-0s, for now our friend found himself in command of a Drummond tank which he shared with his colleagues, and as his eyes took in the well-ordered condition of his footplate he could hardly resist a certain feeling of satisfaction at what he saw. For although the big engines possessed glamour they were not always kept in tip top running order and one never knew from day to day which engine would be rostered. The era of the 'common user' meant working on a wide variety of machines from many depots, engines which received the minimum of care. But now one could be sure that the old Drummond tank would be on the job and she was always in real good nick. Every piece of brasswork on the backplate had been polished while such steel levers as the regulator and reversing handles had been scoured to perfection. Yes, it made quite a difference to the job when you had a regular engine to work with, and a fireman who was keen enough to help keep her in good condition. An approaching rumble broke into our driver's reverie as the down train arrived behind a very grimy mixed traffic 4-6-0 which exuded steam from every possible and improbable place. ("I'm glad I don't have to work on her any more!") A few passengers, some recognisable as regular travellers, climbed aboard the branch train and as the mainliner departed, George the guard looked at his watch, gave a leisurely wave of his flag and it was time to be off. This was the last trip of the day and the journey proceeded on its unruffled way with stops at the two intermediate halts to set down a few passengers at each. On passing the signal box outside the terminus the driver slowed as the fireman leaned out of the cab to pass over the tablet for the single line section to the waiting signalman and then the driver eased his two-coach train into the small oil-lit terminus. It was quite dark by the time the driver had berthed the coaches and the fireman had unhooked the engine and it was but a short while before the 'M7' was alongside the primitive coal stage where Fred, the late-turn shedman could top up the bunker ready for the early morning turn. It took the pair of footplatemen about an hour to 'square up' their engine. The fire had to be dropped into the pit and the ash removed from the smokebox. The driver examined the motion and brake gear, making notes for the fitter concerning the one or two minor defects which would need attention on the morrow. Finally the engine was berthed inside the tiny single-road shed for the night and the driver was free to fill in his Journal, the ticket on which was recorded all of the fireman's and his own activities for the shift. Then after turning off the oil lamps and locking up for the night he made his way home at 11.30 p.m. ("Early turn next week. I still prefer signing on at 5.45 a.m. to these late evening jobs and any way it's better than working the Mail down from Waterloo on a real foggy night with a rough engine. Yes, this isn't a bad life in the main".)

Perhaps in our imagination we might well look back in envy at the life of such a branch line man of twenty or more years ago when steam trains operated on the numerous short branch lines which existed throughout the land. These little lines were often regarded with tolerant amusement by the 'locals', yet there was in fact a great deal of affection for them and now that they are largely gone they are missed for they had been so much a part of the rural scene for the best part of a century. The few that have survived still retain much of the old atmosphere, but somehow the diesel unit does not have the same aura as the steam hauled train, in spite of being faster and cleaner, and also the driver is probably based at a big depot and does not operate exclusively on the one line. Never-the-less, these lines are very much worth a careful study as there are still many remaining associations with former times and soon it may be too late as they are for ever existing under the threat of closure.

This Volume, the third in the Southern Branch Line series, depicts the branches not previously covered. The majority were situated in rural areas and have paid the penalty of unprofitability, but a few have survived into the diesel and electric era. A few shown were freight-only or were constructed for some specific purpose, such as that serving Brookwood cemetery. The editors hope that old memories will be revived and former interests rekindled by the sight of this collection of photographs, while modellers will find help in the very worthwhile task of recreating in miniature their own particular favourite locations. The branches to be found in this volume are: Canterbury-Whitstable; Sandling Junction-Sandgate; Isle of Sheppey lines; Hundred of Hoo lines; Fawkham Jc.-Gravesend West; Paddock Wood-Hawkhurst; Crowhurst-Bexhill West; Lewes-East Grinstead ('Bluebell Line'); Devil's Dyke line; Oxted-Tunbridge Wells West; Deptford Wharf; Newhaven-Seaford; Petersfield-Midhurst; Mid Hants line; Meon Valley line; Botley-Bishop's Waltham; Fovant Military Railway; Brookwood Necropolis line; Brookwood-Bisley; Fawley line; Portland lines; Yeovil lines; Chard Jc.-Chard; Turnchapel line; Bodmin and Wadebridge; Wenford Bridge Mineral line; North Devon and Cornwall Junction line.

Following the gradual silting of the River Stour throughout the eighteenth century, it was decided in 1825 to provide a railway connection between the cathedral city of Canterbury and the River Thames. George Stephenson planned the 6-mile route, the line being built by his assistant, Joseph Locke. The first train, hauled by *Invicta*, ran on 3 May 1830. The harbour was built on the foreshore and sidings, capable of holding some seventy wagons, were laid. Only small coasters could use the harbour; this view, taken on 21 April 1951, shows some of the picturesque Thames barges alongside the quays. [John H. Meredith]

31339
389

The motive power used in the twentieth century was invariably one of the nine specially modified 'R1' 0-6-0Ts. These engines, designed by Stirling as the 'R' Class in 1888, were rebuilt into 'R1's by Wainwright in the early years of this century. In order to clear the restricted Tyler's Hill Tunnel, the branch engines had short stovepipe chimneys, lower domes and pop safety valves, making them easily recognisable. No.31339 is making the climb towards the tunnel with the daily freight on 21 November 1952.
[D.T. Cobbe]

The branch was heavily graded, and loads were limited to 300 tons on these goods trains. Originally there were three halts on the line between Canterbury and Whitstable, and the railway had the distinction of being the first passenger-carrying line in the South of England. However, the passenger services ceased in December 1930, with the freight traffic continuing until 1 December 1952. The 47-ton tank No.31010 leaves the southern end of Tyler's Hill Tunnel on 4 September 1952. A persistent myth states that this tunnel, 828 yards in length, was built at the insistance of the local residents, who felt that every good railway should have one! However, close consideration of the gradient profile of the route, with its climbs of 1 in 50 and even steeper, shows that this tunnel was a physical necessity if the direct route, proposed by promoter William James, was to be adhered to. The principal import at Whitstable was grain to be milled in Ashford, while coal from the local fields was exported. However, as this traffic decreased, the line's fortunes declined and, amid the usual 'last rites', the final goods left Whitstable at 1.00 p.m. on 1 December 1952 behind No.31010, 122 years after its historic opening. [Peter Winding]

Sandling Junction, situated five miles from Folkestone Junction on the Ashford line, marked the connection with the 3½ mile double-line branch to Sandgate, opened on 9 October 1874. This view, taken in S.E.C.R. days, shows a Folkestone to Ashford local in the up main line platform with a Sandgate train at the branch platform. The station was renamed Sandling in 1951 following the closure of the line to the intermediate station of Hythe.
[H.C. Casserley Collection]

A panoramic view of Sandgate station, perched inconveniently above the town, c. 1900. It was originally proposed to extend this line a further three miles to Folkestone Harbour, a scheme which came to nought, yet if it had been completed it would have avoided the building of that operating nightmare, the 1 in 30 incline out of Folkestone Harbour. The Hythe-Sandgate section of the branch was closed on 1 April 1931, an early victim of the motor bus.
[H.C. Casserley Collection]

SITTINGBOURNE
AND MILTON REGIS

KEMSLEY
HALT

Sittingbourne and Milton Regis station, situated on the main L.C.D.R. line, was the original junction for the branch line to Queenborough and Sheerness which was opened to traffic on 19 July 1860. The junction faced Dover, so that through trains from London had to reverse here at Sittingbourne. However, in later years, a spur from West Junction was constructed to allow through running. The branch train waits in the bay on 1 April 1953, with No.31308 at its head, as No.31780 calls with a main line train. [H.C. Casserley]

Another halt was built at the River Swale, 3½ miles from Sittingbourne. Immediately beyond Swale Halt lies the river which separates the Isle of Sheppey from the mainland. The island was reached by the King's Ferry Bridge. The original bridge had a central span which was raised from two towers, thus allowing ships to pass along the waterway. In 1904 a new span of the rolling lift type was installed and served until 1960, when a completely new vertical lift bridge was built alongside the old one. This view, taken on 13 June 1959, shows the new bridge under construction. [Alan A. Jackson]

Kemsley Halt, 2 miles from Sittingbourne, was built in the early years of this century to serve housing developments. This view from the carriage window was taken on 1 April 1953. [H.C. Casserley]

Queenborough station was situated some 2½ miles beyond the bridge. From here a short line to Queenborough Pier was opened in 1876, to be used by boat trains from London which conveyed passengers for the cross-Channel voyage to Flushing. The services ceased at the outbreak of the Great War and were not resumed. Here we see the arrival of one of these trains behind Kirtley 'M2' Class 4-4-0 No.640.
[H.C. Casserley Collection]

The old terminus had two island platforms, which, although grass-grown, may be seen in this view, taken on 13 June 1959. As Sheerness developed into a holiday resort, this site was none too convenient for the newer parts of the town, and so a short extension line was laid to the east of the old station, and a new terminus was built and named Sheerness-on-Sea. [Alan A. Jackson]

The original station at Sheerness, 8 miles from Sittingbourne, was situated near the Naval Dockyard. However, since 1883 this site served as the goods depot for the island. [Alan A. Jackson]

'R1' No.31665 hauls her set of birdcage stock out of Sheerness-on-Sea with the 12.55 p.m. to Sittingbourne on 2 December 1950. [D.T. Cobbe]

The terminus at Sheerness-on-Sea, 1 April 1953, with 'R1' No.31308 in evidence. The centre road acted as a release line for the tank engines which hauled the branch line trains. A frequent service was run, usually up to thirty trains each way, with journey times of some 24 minutes inclusive of stops. [H.C. Casserley]

In 1901 as the prospects of residential development on the east of the Isle of Sheppey seemed favourable, the redoubtable Colonel Stephens constructed the Sheppey Light Railway from Queenborough to Leysdown situated 8¾ miles away on the east coast. The line ran through the outskirts of Sheerness at the East station, seen here on 1 July 1950, with 'E' Class 4-4-0 No.1157 standing at the platform, which was rebuilt in concrete from the original wooden platform during the early 1930s. [D. Trevor Rowe]

31665
SHEERNESS 
EAST

Simple single-platform stations were provided en route from Queenborough at Sheerness East (1½ miles), East Minster (2½ miles), Minster-on-Sea (3¼ miles), Brambledown Halt (4¼ miles), Eastchurch (5½ miles) and Harty Road Halt (7 miles). This view, with 'R1' No.31705, shows the terminus at Leysdown on 2 December 1950. [D.T. Cobbe] Below: No.31698 had the branch duty earlier in the year on 4 March. The articulated set, No.513, is of special interest, as these two vehicles were built as railmotors for the S.E.C.R. in 1905, and probably took their turn in working the line when it opened. Following withdrawal in 1924, Railmotors Nos.1,2,3 and 8 were converted to two articulated sets, Nos.513-4, for use on Sheppey. [D. Trevor Rowe]

BRITISH RAILWAYS

CLOSING OF THE SHEPPEY LIGHT RAILWAY

On and from 4th December, 1950, all services on the above railway between the junction at Queenborough and Leysdown will be withdrawn.

THE FOLLOWING STATIONS WILL BE CLOSED:—

SHEERNESS EAST EASTCHURCH
EAST MINSTER-ON-SEA
HARTY ROAD HALT MINSTER-ON-SEA
LEYSDOWN BRAMBLEDOWN HALT

Omnibus services are operated by the Maidstone and District Motor Services Ltd. between SHEERNESS and the localities now served by the above stations.

Parcels and miscellaneous traffic for cartage by the Railway Executive in the area will be dealt with at Sheerness-on-Sea Station; freight traffic for cartage by the Railway Executive in the area will be dealt with at Sheerness Dockyard Station. Enquiries should be addressed to the Station Master at Sheerness-on-Sea, Tel. Sheerness [illegible] (Parcels, Luggage in Advance, etc.) and 2726 (Freight Traffic).

Facilities for dealing with traffic to be carted by the public exist at Queenborough and Sheerness Stations.

Further information may be obtained from the Divisional Superintendent, British Railways, Orpington—Tel. Orpington [illegible] Ext. 24 or 25.

The 'R1' tanks were long associated with the Sheppey Light Railway. Ordered by S.E.C.R. Locomotive Superintendent Harry Wainwright in 1899, they were a modernised version of Kirtley's 'R' Class of 1891 for the L.C.D.R. Weighing 52 tons, these engines received 'H' Class boilers in later years. As for the Sheppey Light Railway, the traffic never developed to the extent hoped for and the line from Queenborough to Leysdown closed in December 1950. However, the Sheerness branch has fortunately been electrified and continues to provide a regular service including some through trains to and from London. No.31698 is seen at Leysdown on 4 March 1950. [D. Trevor Rowe]

In order to provide communication with that part of North Kent known by its Saxon title of the Hundred of Hoo, a branch was opened in September 1882 from Hoo Junction, 3½ miles east of Gravesend, to Port Victoria, 12¼ miles away on the Isle of Grain. The line had originally only two intermediate stations, at Cliffe (1¾ miles) and Sharnal Street (5¾ miles from Hoo Junction). These had crossing loops and additional platforms on the down side were provided following an increase in traffic in the 1930s. No.31517 is propelling its train from Gravesend in March 1960, while sister engine No.31512 waits in the up platform at Sharnal Street. [Derek Cross]

The first station at Port Victoria was built at the end of a long wooden pier which extended out into the River Medway. It was hoped that a large new docks complex would be developed on this site, but nothing came of this scheme, although paddle steamers did use the pier before the Great War. The pier was shortened in 1916 and this view, taken on 26 April 1930, shows 'H' 0-4-4T No.A311 at the pier station at Port Victoria. In 1931 this station was closed and a simple wooden platform was erected on the land just short of the site of the pier. [H.C. Casserley]

Five additional halts were opened in 1906 at Uralite, High Halstow, Beluncle, Middle Stoke and Grain Crossing. A further halt, at Stoke Junction, was opened in 1932 following the construction of the 1¾-mile long line from that point, some half-a-mile east of Middle Stoke Halt, to Allhallows-on-Sea. A new housing development provided the impetus for this branch and a considerable number of excursion trains were run following its opening on 14 May 1932. This view shows No.31324 approaching Stoke Junction Halt with the local train from Allhallows to Gravesend (Central) on 25 November 1961. [A.E. Bennett]

An island-platform terminus was constructed at Allhallows, and although built as a single track, the line from Stoke Junction was doubled in 1935 because of the increase in traffic. However, the resort did not develop to the extent originally hoped for and the line was singled in 1957. Meanwhile, the traffic to Port Victoria had dwindled to almost nothing, but with the growth of oil refineries at Grain, a new station was opened there in 1951, replacing Port Victoria and Grain Crossing Halt. All passenger services ceased from both Allhallows and Grain on Sunday, 3 December 1961, but freight traffic, including oil, continues to be handled at Grain. This 1959 scene at Allhallows, taken on 13 August, shows No.31517 and a spare coaching set at the platforms. [A.E. Bennett]

51

The 11½-mile branch from Paddock Wood to Hawkhurst was completed by the S.E.R. in 1893. Passing through farmland and hop fields, the line was steeply graded and included a short tunnel some 4½ miles out from Paddock Wood. 'H' Class 0-4-4T No.31324 of Tonbridge shed is seen at Goudhurst, the second station on the line, 6½ miles from Paddock Wood, on 3 June 1961. The station buildings, which include a stationmaster's house, are of typical South Eastern appearance. [A.E. Bennett]

The L.C.D.R. opened a 5-mile long double track branch from Fawkham Junction (situated 5½ miles east of Swanley on the line to Maidstone (East)) to Gravesend (West Street). This line hoped to offer a competitive service to the S.E.R.'s Gravesend traffic and included boat trains to the pier, sited some 150 yards beyond the West Street station. Some continental traffic to Rotterdam was attracted before the Great War, but the branch services were never very well patronised and passenger traffic ceased on 3 August 1953. This view shows 'H' Class 0-4-4T No.31319 at Gravesend (West) in July 1953 at the head of the branch train for Swanley, which would call at Southfleet (2½ miles) and Longfield Halt (4 miles) before reaching the main line. The freight service was withdrawn on 25 March 1968. [Peter Winding]

'D1' 4-4-0 No.31749 pulls away from Cranbrook (10 miles) with a special from London in May 1960. There are several famous boarding schools in the area and these trains were run to coincide with the beginning of the school terms. After unloading at Cranbrook the train proceeded to Hawkhurst, so that the locomotive could run around its stock. [Derek Cross]

The terminus at Hawkhurst (11½ miles). The push-pull unit is in the main platform on 15 August 1959, with the shorter bay visible on the left. The engine neck was just long enough to release a 4-4-0 passenger engine. The passenger traffic dwindled rapidly during the 1950s, partly due to the inconveniently-situated stations being so far from the villages they served and closure came on 12 June 1961. [A.E. Bennett]

A quiet corner at Horsmonden, the first station on the branch, 4 miles from Paddock Wood. The oast houses serve as a reminder of the numerous hop-pickers' specials which used to run before mechanical pickers changed that unique feature of London life.
[A.E. Bennett]

Although Bexhill received its first railway line in 1846, when the L.B.S.C.R. line from Lewes was completed, a further line was opened in 1902 which shortened the journey to London considerably. This was the 4½-mile branch from Crowhurst on the S.E.R. main line to Hastings, which opened on 1 June. Crowhurst station had two bay platforms for accommodating the push-pull trains, which shunted across the four main line tracks between trips. 'H' Class 0-4-4T No.31519 has steam up ready to propel its set out of the downside bay towards Bexhill (West) on 30 May 1958. [Alan A. Jackson]

The line dropped away from Crowhurst and crossed the seventeen-arch viaduct before reaching Sidley, situated 3½ miles from Crowhurst on the outskirts of Bexhill. The station had a small goods shed and siding. No.31279 hurries away towards the terminus one mile away on 22 February 1958. [L.W. Rowe]

Bexhill (West) station was an imposing edifice for a branch terminus, with several sidings for carriages and wagons plus a goods shed. The signal box visible in front of the station clock was replaced by a new box in the station yard. The branch engine on duty on 7 August 1956 is No.31519. [A.E. Bennett]

St. Leonards shed (74E) usually had a half-dozen of the useful 'H' tanks on its strength for local duties. Two were rostered for the Bexhill branch trips, the service being eleven journeys each way in the latter years of steam operation. The workings were dieselised in June 1958 following the introduction of the main line diesel-electric units on the Hastings service. However, the branch was one of the first to suffer from the Beeching Plan and closed for freight on 9 September 1963 and passengers on 15 June 1964. No.31269 is in charge of the branch train at Bexhill (West) on 30 June 1956. [H.C. Casserley]

The 17-mile Lewes and East Grinstead Railway was opened to traffic on 1 August 1882. Amalgamated with the L.B.S.C.R., the line ran from Culver Junction, 3 miles north of Lewes on the Uckfield line, to a newly constructed station at East Grinstead. This was the Low Level, built beneath and at right angles to the High Level platforms of the Horsham – Tunbridge Wells line. This view, looking south past the small Saxby and Farmer signal box, shows Ivatt Class '2' 2-6-2T No.41299 at the head of a Lewes train on 7 April 1956.
[C.E. Dann]

An Act of Parliament allowed the closure of the line's passenger services on 17 March 1958, but the line continued to see some activity. Class '4' 2-6-4T No.80138 rumbles through Kingscote (2 miles from East Grinstead) with a load of condemned wagons in April 1960.
[Derek Cross]

Passenger services on the route, known as the 'Bluebell Line', were scheduled to cease on 13 June 1955. However, it was discovered that in the original amalgamation agreement the L.B.S.C.R. had to allow four trains per day at certain stations, so the service was resumed on 7 August 1956. 'C2x' 0-6-0 goods No.32442 of Brighton shed was allocated the passenger duty in October 1956 and waits in the Low Level for the 'right-away' from the guard.
[C.E. Dann]

'C2x' No.32442 pauses at West Hoathly (4 miles) with its two-coach set, October 1956. Originally the line boasted eleven signal boxes between Culver Junction and East Grinstead, but four sufficed in S.R. days, one being situated at this station. [C.E. Dann]

The station buildings and fine old wooden overbridge (unfortunately long since demolished) at West Hoathly, April 1955. The tunnel, seen beyond Ivatt tank No. 41299, is 730 yards long. [C.E. Dann]

The 11.33 a.m. Lewes to East Grinstead heads north out of West Hoathly behind No.32442 on 6 October 1956. The goods siding, significantly empty, is situated at this northern end of the station. [R.K. Taylor]

HORSTED KEYNES

R.C.T.S.
THE
WEALDEN LIMITED
RCTS
RCTS
32426

'Old Faithful' No.32442 yet again at work on the Bluebell trains, seen at Horsted Keynes on 7 August 1956. This engine crew have not put down the storm sheet for the tender-first running. Perhaps the bean sticks are due for a journey to their new home on the locomotive's tender! [A.E. Bennett]

From West Hoathly Tunnel, the double-track line dropped at 1 in 75 to the imposing station at Horsted Keynes. Although serving a small village, this station had an air of importance, as it was the junction for the short line to Haywards Heath. This view, on 3 March 1934, shows 'D1' tank No.2284 in the down branch platform with another local train in the up branch platform. The line on the left was the original down main, with the up main on the other platform face, but this latter was removed and the former became the up main, being the end of the 1935 electrification from Haywards Heath. [H.C. Casserley]

The route via Horsted Keynes and Haywards Heath was often used as an alternative to the Brighton main line, especially during the Second World War. This 1955 scene serves as a reminder of such traffic with that great Brighton veteran, 'H2' Atlantic No.32426 *St. Alban's Head*, at the head of the R.C.T.S. 'Wealden Limited' Railtour. [D. Trevor Rowe]

Four-and-a-half miles south of Horsted Keynes lies Sheffield Park. There were once two sidings serving timber and milk depots, plus two signal boxes, though these were replaced in Southern days by a groundframe. The main locomotive water supply for the line was situated here, although there was also a somewhat inadequate supply at Horsted Keynes. The upper picture shows the station, looking north, while below, Ivatt Class '2' 2-6-2T No.41299 waits with a southbound train as a Fairburn 2-6-4T eases into the up platform on 7 April 1956. [C.E. Dann]

After passing Newick and Chailey (12½ miles from East Grinstead) the southbound train reaches Barcombe (16 miles). No.32536 is seen heading north near Barcombe with the 3.30 p.m. from Lewes on 6 October 1956.
[R.K. Taylor]

The 4¾-mile line from Horsted Keynes to Haywards Heath (opened 3 September 1883) had one 218-yard tunnel and an intermediate station at Ardingly (2¼ miles). Electrified in 1935, the passenger service ceased in October 1963. Lawson Billinton's 'K' Class Mogul No.32343 is heading a condemned wagon train through from Horsted Keynes in March 1960.
[Derek Cross]

80152
75A
SC

The 2.28 p.m. East Grinstead-Lewes train at Sheffield Park station on 1 March 1958 with one engine, Standard Class '4' 2-6-4T No.80152, one coach, No.S3847S, one engine crew, one guard, one spectator and only one passenger (the photographer). Such was the state of the Bluebell line shortly before closure. However, the Bluebell Railway Preservation Society was formed in 1959 and on 17 May 1960 the first engine and carriages arrived on its line, which ran from Sheffield Park to a point 279 yards short of Horsted Keynes. Following the cessation of B.R.'s service, access to Horsted Keynes was obtained and, at the time of writing, the Company has had nineteen years of successful operation.
[Hugh Ballantyne]

In 1888 the L.B.S.C.R. opened a line from Hurst Green Junction (near Oxted) to Ashurst Junction, which allowed direct running from Oxted to Tunbridge Wells by a much shorter route than that via East Grinstead. The line was double throughout and some through trains from Victoria to Tunbridge Wells (West) were run, but the majority of trains were locals between the latter town and Oxted. Above: No.31520 enters Groombridge on an Oxted push-pull service, June 1961. Below: No.31005 pauses at the rural station of Ashurst (2½ miles north of Groombridge) on 1 June 1962. The gas lamps and the old lady add an air of a bygone age, in keeping with the elderly locomotive. [A.R. Butcher]

The 3½-mile branch from Dyke Junction, near Aldrington Halt on the main line west of Hove, to Devil's Dyke on the South Downs, was opened on 1 September 1887. The line was heavily graded, rising over 400′ at a ruling gradient of 1 in 40, while sharp reverse curves abounded. The line was closed from 1917 to 1920, and during the 1930s many of the trains from Brighton terminated at Rowan Halt, half-a-mile beyond the branch junction. The porter/signalman is taking the single-line staff from the fireman of the Stroudley 'D1' at Dyke station in May 1927. The line closed on the last day of 1938, the final train being the 5.37 p.m. from Dyke, hauled by 'E4' No.2505. So great were the numbers of passengers that a three-coach S.E.C.R. set was added to the ex-L.B.S.C.R. centre-corridor 'Balloon' coach which usually sufficed on this service. Today it is difficult to get a bus to the Dyke – 'Fine days in Summer only!' [Late W.B. Bushell Collection]

31005

Two-and-a-half miles north of Ashurst lies Cowden station, then comes Hever, 2 miles nearer Oxted. The station view at Hever above was taken in April 1969, in post-steam days. [C.E. Dann]

However, steam is much in evidence in this March 1960 scene, as No.31306 pulls away with its S.E.R. set. [Derek Cross

A close-up of the Brighton oil lamp on the platform at Hever station in April 1969.
[C.E. Dann]

The S.E.R. opened its Edenbridge station (on the Redhill-Tonbridge line) in 1842. The Brighton station, seen here in June 1960, was opened on 2 January 1888, the most important location on the 12½-mile line. The freight facilities were withdrawn from this station in 1968. No.31544 is steaming well as she leaves the down platform.
[Derek Cross]

31544
31544
300

48 A number of Fairburn-designed 2-6-4 tanks of L.M.S. origins worked in the Tunbridge Wells area. No.42103 is seen leaving Hurst Green Halt (closed in June 1961) in June 1953 with a London Bridge to East Grinstead stopper. Note the fine pair of wooden-posted L.B.S.C.R. lower quadrant signals, the one on the extreme right being that for the line from Ashurst Junction, the Fairburn tank being on the older line to East Grinstead. [C.E. Dann]

'H' Class No.31543 has full steam raised (160lbs. per sq.in.) ready to propel her set out of Oxted's bay platform towards Tunbridge Wells (West) on 14 December 1961. [A.R. Butcher]

No.31005 bowls along near Monk's Lane Halt (11 miles from Groombridge and closed in September 1939) on 1 June 1962. The 'H' Class tanks have featured frequently on the branch lines depicted so far. Designed by Harry Wainwright in 1904, 66 of these 54-ton 0-4-4Ts were built in Ashford Works up until 1915. They were highly successful in service, first on the heavy suburban trains and later on such country branch duties as these. Also they enjoyed considerable popularity among the enginemen, including those of the Brighton section, who took to these 'foreigners' with enthusiasm. [A.R. Butcher]

The L.B.S.C.R. had its own dock facilities on the banks of the Thames at Deptford. A branch was constructed from the Company's main depot at New Cross Gate and a considerable tonnage of traffic was handled before the Second World War. The line passed under the main Brighton tracks and then crossed the Surrey Canal by way of a lifting bridge. Drummond 'M7' No.30050 pauses on this bridge during the course of an East London railtour on 31 May 1959. [A.E. Bennett]

The branch line passed under the S.E.R. main line before crossing the public highway at Grove Road and entered the yards at Deptford Wharf. These docks were once well-equipped with hydraulic cranes and electric traversers, and handled imports of coal for the nearby gas works as well as timber, grain, flour and other commodities. Numerous railwaymen and dockers worked here but with the rapid decline in river traffic during the last two decades, the Wharf has suffered the same fate as other establishments in East London's Dockland. However, a fair amount of traffic is in evidence on the occasion of the railtour visit of 31 May 1959. [A.E. Bennett]

The railway first reached the tidal port of Newhaven in 1847 and a 2½-mile extension was continued to Seaford and opened on 1 June 1864. As the traffic increased the line was doubled in 1905. There is one intermediate halt at Bishopstone. The line was electrified as part of the Central Section's Hastings scheme of 1935. A railtour on 7 October 1962 revived memories of earlier days when small Brighton tanks worked the service, as 'Terrier' No.32636 and 'E6' 0-6-2T No.32418 were the selected motive power. [Peter Paye]

The special train passes Newhaven en route for Seaford. This view illustrates how diminutive the 'Terriers' really were, as the 'E6' is not a very large locomotive, yet it seems to tower over the former engine. A new and larger station was opened at Seaford when the line was doubled and the traffic remained constant for many years, although the town of Seaford itself has not grown to any great extent. In recent years, the branch trains have run from Seaford to Lewes or Brighton and numbered up to 35 departures from Seaford on weekdays. [G.D. King]

Three lines converged on the town of Midhurst. The first proposal was the Mid-Sussex and Midhurst (see Volume 2), which finally reached the town in October 1866, being worked by the Brighton. From the opposite direction, the L.S.W.R. proposed a line from Petersfield on the Portsmouth Direct line and this was opened on 1 September 1864, two years before the line from Pulborough. The first station on the South Western route was Rogate for Harting, 4½ miles from Petersfield. (The third line was the 1881 branch from Chichester, also noted in Volume 2).

[D. Trevor Rowe/ H.C. Casserley]

Drummond 'M7' No.30049 is about to push its two-coach L.S.W.R. set out of Elsted (6¼ miles from Petersfield), working the 10.41 a.m. Pulborough to Petersfield on 5 February 1955. For many years the Adams 'T1' 0-4-4 tanks worked from the Petersfield end of the line, but in the post-War years Drummond tanks predominated, working from Horsham and Guildford sheds.
[D.T. Cobbe]

Elsted Station, 20 September 1952.
[H.C. Casserley]

The old L.S.W.R. station at Midhurst, July 1951. This station was some distance from that on the Pulborough line, and a short spur was laid in December 1866 to allow through running. After Grouping, this station was closed in 1925 and all passenger traffic was concentrated at the Brighton station, although the L.S.W.R. goods shed remained in service for some while longer. [Peter Winding]

Drummond 'M7' tank No.130 waits in the bay at Midhurst, 30 October 1928. The station, of typical Brighton architectural style, boasted a refreshment room in those far-off days. [H.C. Casserley]

'M7', No.30108, steams away from Midhurst towards the tunnel with the 2.45 p.m. to Pulborough on Christmas Day, 1954 [D. Trevor Rowe]

Another motor-fitted 'M7' No.30027 prepares to leave Midhurst with the 10.40 a.m. Petersfield to Pulborough on 19 January 1952. A service of eight trains each way was run between Petersfield and Pulborough, but this was terminated on 7 February 1955 and the lines closed entirely on 12 October 1964. [D.T. Cobbe]

The Alton, Alresford and Winchester Railway (later named Mid-Hants Railway) opened for traffic on 2 October 1865. The first station at Alton (seen above in 1959) was the original terminus of the line from Guildford, opened in 1852; a new station was built on the extension and the original was used as the goods depot. [Peter Winding]. Below: Although envisaged as an alternative through route from Waterloo, the Mid Hants remained essentially a branch line. However, when diversions from the main Southampton line were necessary, particularly during the electrification works of the 1960s, the steep 1 in 66 climb to Medstead echoed to the sound of hard-pressed main line engines. No less a train than the 'Bournemouth Belle' is seen in action behind 'U' No.31628 and 'M.N.' No.35026 *Lamport and Holt Line* on 17 July 1966. [L. Elsey]

Medstead (4¼ miles) was not opened until three years after the rest of the line. Goods traffic was withdrawn in 1964 and complete closure came, following the withdrawal of all services from the line, on 5 February 1973.
[A.E. Bennett]

Ropley was situated another 3¼ miles down the track. A crossing loop existed here until its removal in 1931.
[A.E. Bennett]

Alresford, 10 miles from Alton, was the largest station on the line, with a crossing loop and two platforms retained. A small goods yard remained in service until 1964, when all freight traffic on the line was suspended.
[A.E. Bennett]

Itchen Abbas, 3½ miles from Alresford and 3¼ miles from Winchester Junction, was of similar architectural style to the other stations on the line and once maintained a crossing loop (until 1921) and goods yard until 1962.
[A.E. Bennett]

Snow-plough fitted 'M7' No.30479 awaits the right-away at Alresford on 3 September 1955. Not for nothing was the Mid Hants line known as 'Over the Alps' to the footplatemen from Eastleigh and Guildford sheds who worked the services. Long stretches of 1 in 80 and 1 in 60 caused many headaches, but the Drummond tanks, with the earlier Adams 'T1's and later diesel-electric units, battled up and down the numerous banks. Fortunately, there is still activity at Alresford, as the present-day Mid-Hants Company operates several locomotives, including Maunsell Mogul No.31874, from Alresford station, re-opened on 30 April 1977. Over 50,000 people were carried on the 3-mile section between Alresford and Ropley in the Company's first season.

[Hugh Ballantyne]

A short branch line just over 3½ miles in length was opened from Botley to Bishop's Waltham on the Eastleigh – Fareham line on 6 June 1863. Adams '02' 0-4-4 tank No.236 stands in the branch line platform at Botley on 7 November 1928.
[H.C. Casserley]

The Bishop's Waltham line curves away to the north from the main line at Botley, 7 March 1959.
[A.E. Bennett]

Drummond 'M7' No.30111 stands in the disused station at Bishop's Waltham with a railtour on 7 March 1959. Traffic was never heavy on this branch and the passenger services were withdrawn as early as 2 January 1933, but goods traffic continued until 30 April 1962, when the line was closed completely. [A.E. Bennett]

Drummond '700' Class 0-6-0 goods engine No.30698 at Alton after working a freight duty on the Meon Valley line, 28 May 1956. These 43-ton (plus 36-ton tender) engines were built by Dubs of Glasgow in 1897 to Dugald Drummond's design for service as heavy goods locomotives on the L.S.W.R. Although all thirty members of the class were superheated by Urie and Maunsell, they were superseded on the heaviest duties by 4-6-0s, but were often rostered for branch freight duties until the early 1960s. [Hugh Ballantyne]

The 22¼-mile Meon Valley line, between Alton and Farnham, was opened to traffic on 1 June 1903. The line was envisaged as an alternative through route to such coastal locations as Gosport, but in reality very little long distance traffic passed over the line. Farringdon, 3¼ miles south of Alton, was originally only a goods depot, but in 1931 the passenger platform was added – a reversal of the usual branch line procedures! However, the station reverted to freight-only status on 7 February 1955 and closed entirely on 5 August 1968. This view was taken on 21 September 1958. [Alan A. Jackson]

Tisted station, facing towards Alton, 5¼ miles away, on 9 August 1954. The line was single track although embankments and cuttings were to double-track standards and all stations had double platforms with passing loops. However, the grass-grown surfaces show how sparse the passenger traffic had become in later years. [R.M. Casserley]

Three-and-a-quarter miles farther south was Privett, again looking unkept and desolate when seen from the windows of a passing train on 9 August 1954. One of the main engineering features of the line, a 1,056-yard tunnel, was located near this station. [R.M. Casserley]

TRAIN SERVICE
TRAIN SERVICE
363
FPM 797

The R.C.T.S. 'Hampshireman' Railtour hauled by Nos.30301 and 30732 at West Meon (12½ miles from Alton) on 6 February 1955. Although the notice boards advertise the train service, in actual fact the public passenger trains made their last runs on the previous day. A short way to the north of this station lay a 539-yard tunnel. [Hugh Ballantyne]

Another 4 miles to the south lay the station of Droxford. This 1962 view, taken seven years after the cessation of the passenger services, shows the 600ft. platforms which were provided here and at the other stations in anticipation of the arrival of lengthy trains. [H.C. Casserley]

Droxford station on 7 March 1959 with a railtour headed by 'M7' No.30111, making a stop for the benefit of the photographers. The majority of trains in later years were made up of motor-fitted push and pull units with 'M7's in charge. [A.E. Bennett]

Freight traffic continued to be handled at Farringdon and Droxford until 5 August 1968. This view at Wickham (21½ miles from Alton) shows 'U' Class 2-6-0 No.31618 of Eastleigh shed with the Droxford goods on 27 April 1962. The paucity of the merchandise carried is only too obvious. [H.C. Casserley]. Below: the remains of Wickham station (facing towards Alton) 27 April 1962. As the line from Fareham to Droxford by that date was no longer a public route, it was little more than a long siding and was not signalled, being run on the 'one engine in steam' principle. The line continued past Knowle Halt (23 miles) to Fareham (25¾ miles from Alton). [H.C. Casserley]

Not strictly a Southern line, but in L.S.W.R. territory, was the Fovant Military Railway. Opened in 1915, this line ran from Dinton, on the Salisbury to Yeovil main line, to the great encampment at Fovant, 2 miles to the south. The saddle tank, seen at Fovant, is named *Hampshire*, while below is one of the Adams Radial tanks which were 'called up' during the Great War. It is known that No.424 was a regular performer on the line, but close scrutiny with the magnifying glass seems to reveal the number 417. The line closed soon after the Armistice.

[A.C.V. Kendall Collection]

The London Necropolis Company established a vast cemetery on the south side of the L.S.W.R. main line some 3 miles west of Woking at Brookwood. In order to provide transport from the capital into the cemetery, the Company constructed a three-quarter mile branch from the main line to the west of what became Brookwood station (which was built at the Company's expense in 1864). The Cemetery Railway opened in 1854 and a terminal was built close to Waterloo station by the L.S.W.R. Trains ran when required, often twice weekly, and in the 1930s were usually hauled by 'M7' tanks which ran around the stock at Brookwood before entering the cemetery. There were two stations, the North (above) and South (below), each situated either side of the Brookwood – Pirbright road which bisects the cemetery. These views, with 'M7' No.244 on show, were taken on 30 May 1930. The service ceased in May 1941 when bombing destroyed the London terminal, and was never resumed.

[H.C. Casserley]

Another short branch was laid from Brookwood to Bisley at the behest of the National Rifle Association. Opened on 14 July 1890, trains ran when meetings were held and of course during the two Wars, when thousands of men trained on the rifle ranges. No.30108 is in the bay at Brookwood with the branch train (Set No.734, coupe S4759 and 3rd control S2644) on 18 July 1952. [John H. Meredith]

The view from the last train out of Bisley, prior to departure on 23 November 1952.
[Hugh Ballantyne]

HYTHE

A close-up of No.30032 after arrival at the terminus. The passenger service was closed down on 14 February 1966 and public freight handling had ceased on the branch by 1967, but the vast oil refinery at Fawley generates a great volume of traffic and numerous block oil trains pass over the line en route to a variety of destinations throughout Britain. These trains are now usually hauled by Classes '33' or '47' diesels. [A.E. Bennett]

The branch from Eling Junction (just west of Totton on the Southampton – Bournemouth line) to Fawley, on Southampton Water, was opened as a light railway by the S.R. on 20 July 1925. Great hopes of growth were expressed at that time, with possible through traffic to the Isle of Wight and seaside developments on the Solent, but the passenger traffic consisted largely of workmen's trains to the oil refinery at Fawley. The first station was at Marchwood, 3½ miles from Eling. No.30032 is seen at the second station, Hythe (6½ miles), on 11 July 1959. [A.E. Bennett]

No.30032 has arrived at Fawley, the terminus 8¾ miles from Eling. Most of the passenger trains originated at Eastleigh or Southampton and numbered only four or five a day. [A.E. Bennett]

The Weymouth and Portland line opened on 16 October 1865 and was leased jointly to the G.W.R. and L.S.W.R. The line originally left the main line station at Weymouth, but a small platform was opened at Melcombe Regis, just short of the junction and close to Weymouth station, in 1909. With steam and smoke seen rising from the Western loco depot at Weymouth in the background, Adams '02' No.229 enters Melcombe Regis with Western stock in tow on 4 June 1949. [John H. Meredith]

The line was extended from Portland to Easton in 1900, with the passenger service commencing on 1 September 1902. Use was made of earlier mineral lines on this new section. Stations existed at Westham (one quarter-mile), Rodwell (three-quarter mile), Sandsfoot Castle (1¼-mile), Wyke Regis (2¼ miles), Portland (4¼ miles), and Easton (8¾ miles). '02' No.30177 is seen in the terminus on 16 February 1952, shortly before closure took place on 3 March. [John H. Meredith]

The first railway at Yeovil was the branch from Durston, near Taunton, which reached a terminus at Hendford on the outskirts of the town. A further G.W.R. line was opened to Pen Mill in 1856 as part of the main line from Frome to Weymouth. The L.S.W.R. line from Salisbury reached Hendford on 1 June 1860, but seven weeks later the main line from Yeovil Junction to Exeter was opened and Yeovil became a 'branch line town' as far as the South Western was concerned. A new joint station used by trains from Durston, Pen Mill and Yeovil Junction was opened in 1861 and it is at this station, Yeovil Town, that No.30129 is seen on 31 August 1960 with the auto-train working the service to the junction. [John Goss]

A flash-back to 21 May 1935 with a stranger, ex-L.B.S.C.R. 'D1' 0-4-2T No.2273, at work with the auto-train composed of former steam railmotor cars. The junction was 1¾ miles from the Town station.
[H.C. Casserley]

Western Region assumed responsibility for all lines west of Salisbury in 1963 and as a consequence W.R. locomotives were often seen on former Southern preserves. Pannier tank No.5416 approaches Yeovil Town from the Junction with W.R. stock on 23 June 1963. The line to the left leads to Pen Mill station on the Weymouth line. Today, the Junction and Pen Mill stations remain open, but the Town station closed on 2 October 1966 and freight services at Hendford and the Town ceased in October 1967.
[G.D. King]

he L.S.W.R. constructed a 3¼-mile branch from Chard Junction, on the Yeovil – Exeter line, to Chard in 363, while the G.W.R. opened a line from Taunton on 11 September 1866. The two companies used a joint ation at Chard (Central) and eventually the L.S.W.R. terminus, seen here on 23 August 1958, was closed on January 1917 and used as the freight depot. Also from that date the Western took over all train operation n the line from Taunton to Chard Junction. [A.E. Bennett]. Below: the Southern station at Chard Junction in e 1930s. This was closed for main line traffic in March 1966, the branch line having closed for passengers n 10 September 1962 and for freight in 1966. [A. Fairclough Collection]

In 1891 the L.S.W.R. opened a new terminus in eastern Plymouth at Friary. Six years later, on 1 September 1897, a branch was opened from the main line three-quarters of a mile from Friary which, having crossed the River Plym by way of the swing bridge, proceeded towards Turnchapel, 2½ miles from Friary. Motor-fitted '02' No.233 is seen propelling its set of converted steam railcars towards Friary on 14 June 1926. On board the tank the fireman may be seen bending to his lonely task, with his mate in the driving compartment of the leading vehicle. The lattice metal gates on the open gangways of the stock also show up well. To the right may be seen the wagons in Bayly's timber yard which is served by the Cattewater freight branch.
[H.C. Casserley]

The Turnchapel line closed for passengers on 10 September 1951, but old times were revived on 2 May 1959 with the sight of an '02', No.30182, at the Turnchapel terminus, when a R.C.T.S. special traversed the branch. The branch actually continued as a single line for a further half-mile in order to serve freight sidings. A halt existed at Oreston (2 miles from Friary), while the branch trains also called at Lucas Terrace Halt (half-mile), situated on the main line close to the Turnchapel junction. [R.M. Casserley]

The R.C.T.S. special, complete with L.S.W.R. gated stock, calls at Plymstock (1½ miles). This was the junction for the G.W.R. branch to Yealmpton, which opened on 17 January 1898 and finally closed on 7 October 1947, having also shut down from 7 July 1930 to 3 November 1941. Of course, trains of both companies used the swing bridge. Freight traffic on the line ceased on 2 October 1961. [R.M. Casserley]

The Bodmin & Wadebridge Railway, opened on 30 September 1834, was one of the earliest railways in the world. Stations were situated at Grogley (3 miles), Nanstallon (4½ miles), Dunmere (5¼ miles) and Bodmin North (6¾ miles from Wadebridge). A main line connection, albeit to the Great Western main line, was obtained in 1887 from Boscarne Junction to Bodmin Road, and in 1895 the L.S.W.R.'s North Cornwall line reached Wadebridge, thus connecting this isolated branch with the Company's main system. The last steam locomotives to work the passenger services were Ivatt's successful 2-6-2 tanks; No.41320 is at Bodmin North on 13 May 1963.
[J.R. Besley]

The Adams '02' tanks worked the Bodmin branch for many years, their final fling being in the early 1960s. These 47-ton tanks, costing £1500 when first introduced in 1889, worked many of the lighter branch line duties on the Western Section of the Southern, and were also the mainstay of the Isle of Wight services for forty years. No.203 worked from Wadebridge shed for a number of years along with a sister engine, and is seen at her home station on 29 August 1945. This particular engine was one of several fitted with a Drummond replacement boiler.
[H.C. Casserley]

A picturesque mineral line ran from Dunmere Junction (5 miles from Wadebridge) to Wenford Bridge (12 miles). Originally constructed for the transport of sand inland, this line has continued to prosper through the shipment of china clay from the dries at Wenford. From 1895 the line was worked by Beattie 2-4-0 well tanks, three of which survived until 1962, when for a short while ex-G.W.R. '1366' tanks were used pending the arrival of diesel shunters. No.30587 is seen in the clay sidings at Wenford on 27 March 1962.

[K.J. Marden].

N.B. For a full description of this unique line see Bradford Barton's 'Bodmin & Wadebridge Railway' in this pictorial series.

41297

Busy activity at Torrington in April 1963. The 12.10 p.m. goods prepares to leave behind No.41213, with the Barnstaple and London train backing into the up platform, while a 'West Country' marshalls carriages in the down sidings. The milk tanks on the right have been filled at the large processing plant. [Peter Paye]

The L.S.W.R. reached Torrington in 1872, trains running via Barnstaple and Exeter to London. On 27 July 1925 a 20½-mile extension, the North Devon and Cornwall Junction Railway, was opened to traffic, this being one of the last lines of any length to be constructed in Britain. This scene at Torrington on Saturday, 8 April 1961 shows Ivatt Class '2' No.41313 ready to depart with the 12.18 p.m. The first vehicle is a green Bulleid BCK for Waterloo, next L.M.S. six-wheel Guard's Brake BGZ and then three maroon G.W.R. carriages for Taunton. [J.R. Besley]

With the train described above still in the platform, No.41297 prepares to leave Torrington with the 12.10 p.m. goods to Halwill. The newspaper van from London may be seen in the goods shed on the right. [J.R. Besley]

No.41213 again works the 12.10 p.m. to Halwill out of Torrington in August 1963. The open wagons are used for the transport of clay from the North Devon Clay Company's Marland works near Meeth.
[Peter Paye]

The 1.55 p.m. mixed train from Petrockstow makes its lonely way through the beautiful North Devon countryside near Torrington behind No.41210 in August 1963. [Peter Paye]

No.41298 plus one carriage leaves Watergate (1¼ miles) on 16 April 1955. Another halt was situated at Yarde (4½ miles). [J.R. Besley]

No.41294 crosses the River Torridge at Torrington with the mixed train from Petrockstow on 29 August 1959. This station lies in the river valley only 77 ft. above sea level. The other end of the line at Halwill is at an altitude of over 600 ft., so the heavy gradients may be imagined. [D. Trevor Rowe]

After climbing at 1 in 45 away from the Torridge the line drops down to Dunsbear Halt (5¾ miles). No.41299 pauses with the train from Halwill on 28 August 1962.
[Pamlin Prints]

Petrockstow (10 miles) was provided with a crossing loop where trains could pass. No.41283 on the 4.00 p.m. from Torrington is crossing the 4.37 p.m. to Torrington in August 1963. This locomotive is fitted with the wide Ivatt chimney originally designed for this class which first appeared on the L.M.S. in 1946. [Peter Paye]

A Halwill to Torrington train calls at Meeth (10¾ miles from Torrington) on 28 August 1962.
[Pamlin Prints]

A Torrington-bound train at Hatherleigh platform on 28 May 1956. The cattle trucks serve as a reminder of the livestock once transported to and from such market towns by our railways, this part of Devon being real cattle country. Over 8,000 animals per year were carried on this line during the 1950s. Unfortunately this station was sited some 2 miles from the town, which restricted its use by would-be travellers. [H.C. Casserley]

Another view of Meeth Halt with No.41298 in charge of a short freight on 14 August 1956. This engine was one of those built with the tall narrow design of chimney developed after the draughting tests carried out at the Swindon Works of Western Region. There were a number of ungated level crossings on this line, these requiring rigid observance of the 10 m.p.h. speed restrictions. [R.E. Toop]

No.41283 with the 4.00 p.,m. at Hole (17¾ miles). The N.D.C.J. Railway was built at a time of great unemployment and the Government gave a grant of £125,000, almost half the total cost of the line, in order to provide some much-needed work in the area. Unfortunately the line, with a ruling gradient of 1 in 50 and numerous curves and climbs, did not prosper to the extent of early hopes. [Peter Paye]

No.41283 at Hatherleigh with the 4.00 p.m. Torrington to Halwill in August 1963. Water columns were provided here, although the Ivatts, with their 1,350-gallon capacity, were usually able to run through to Torrington or Halwill. These engines, weighing 63 tons, had a tractive effort of 17,400lbs. and were a considerable advance on the L.B.S.C.R. 'E1R' 0-6-2Ts which worked the line from the late 1920s to the late 1950s. [Peter Paye]

The end of the line at Halwill. The platform on the extreme left was built in 1925 to accommodate the Light Railway trains. The line second from left is that from Bude, while 'N' Class 2-6-0 No.31856 is at the head of the 1.05 p.m. from Padstow (17 August 1963). This train will pass over the crossover into the up platform, the fireman being ready with the tablet in his hands. The branch line closed throughout from Torrington (and indeed from Barnstaple) on 4 October 1965, while the Bude and Padstow lines followed suit one year later on 3 October 1966. [Peter Paye]

MIDLAND
NORTH EASTERN
STEAM
GREAT WESTERN
STEAM MISCELLANY
BODMIN AND WADEBRIDGE
GREAT WESTERN
BRANCH LINE STEAM
BRITISH
NARROW GAUGE
STEAM
STANDARD
STEAM
IN ACTION
DIESELS
ON SCOTTISH REGION
BR DIESELS
IN THE
LANDSCAPE
BR DIESELS
IN ACTION
H. C. CASSERLEY
IRISH RAILWAYS
in the heyday of steam
SOUTHERN
THE LYNTON &
BARNSTAPLE
RAILWAY
THE WARSHIPS
THE WAINWRIGHT CLASSES
STEAM
NORTH EASTERN
STEAM
LONDON MIDLAND
STEAM IN ACTION 4
CLASS 42/43 DIESEL-HYDRAULICS
THE LONDON RT BUS
SOUTHERN STEAM
STANIER 8F
2-8-0
GREAT
CENTRAL
recalled
GEORGE DOW
STEAM